THE

OF OZ

Original Work by L. Frank Baum
Retold by Pauline Francis
Illustrated by Mike Spoor

Steck
Vaughn™

A Harcourt Education Imprint
www.Steck-Vaughn.com
1-800-531-5015

The Wizard of Oz

Steck-Vaughn Fast Track Classics

First published by Evans Brothers Limited (a member of the Evans Publishing Group)
Copyright © Evans Brothers Limited 2007
This edition published under license from Evans Brothers Limited
This edition copyright © 2008 Harcourt Achieve Inc.

Harcourt Achieve Inc.
10801 N. MoPac Expy., Bldg. 3
Austin, TX 78759
www.harcourtachieve.com

ISBN-13: 978-1-4190-5091-6
ISBN-10:   1-4190-5091-5

Steck-Vaughn is a trademark of Harcourt Achieve Inc.

Printed in China

1 2 3 4 5 6 7 8 985 14 13 12 11 10 09 08 07

THE WIZARD OF OZ

Introduction

Lyman Frank Baum was born in 1856 in New York, one of seven brothers and sisters. His father owned many businesses and theaters. At the age of seventeen, Baum became a reporter for the *New York World* magazine.

Baum married at the age of twenty-six and had four sons. He earned his living in many ways: as a salesman for his father, as a magazine journalist, and as a writer.

The Wonderful Wizard of Oz was published in 1900 and is Baum's best-known book for children. It tells the story of a girl named Dorothy who is blown to the Land of Oz by a tornado. She sets off to find the Wizard of Oz to ask him to help her return home. As she walks along a yellow brick road, she meets some strange characters.

L. Frank Baum wrote in 1900: *"I wrote this book just to please children. I have tried to make it a modern fairy tale, but I have left out the horrors of the older fairy tales."*

The book was turned into a musical and made a film many times. The most famous film was *The Wizard of Oz*, which was released in 1939. The film had several differences from the book, one of the more memorable ones being the change of Dorothy's silver shoes to ruby slippers.

L. Frank Baum died in 1919, at his home, called Ozcot, in Hollywood.

CHAPTER ONE

The Tornado

A young girl named Dorothy went to live with her aunt and uncle because she was an orphan. They lived on a farm right in the middle of the Kansas prairie. There were no trees or other houses, just the baking hot sun, the whistling wind—and the tornadoes that often blew across this part of America.

One day, the sky was grayer than usual. From the north came the wail of the wind. The corn swayed. Then the air from the south whistled.

"There's a tornado coming, Em," Uncle Henry shouted to his wife. "I'm going to check on the cattle. You take Dorothy down to the cellar."

Aunt Em was so frightened that she ran to the cellar, leaving Dorothy to follow her. As Dorothy went to pick up Toto, a little black dog, the wind shook the house hard. Then a strange thing happened. The house whirled around and around and rose slowly into the air.

"I'll stay here and see what happens," Dorothy told herself as she sat down on the floor.

Hour after hour, the house moved and swayed gently, until Dorothy fell asleep. Suddenly, the house gave a big jolt and Toto began to whine. Dorothy woke up. She opened the door, and bright sunshine flooded the little house.

"Look, Toto!" Dorothy cried. "It's beautiful out there! There are fruit trees and flowers and birds!"

As she watched, strange people gathered around the house. They were small—as big as Dorothy—but older than her, and they wore pointed hats with bells around the brim. The men wore blue and the women wore white. An old woman came up to the door of the house.

"Welcome to the land of the Munchkins," she said. "Thank you for killing the witch. You have set them all free."

Dorothy was surprised. "But I haven't killed anybody!" she cried.

The old woman pointed to the corner of the house. "Those are the witch's feet," she said. "Your house fell on her."

"Oh dear!" Dorothy said, her heart beating faster. "Who was she? And who are you?"

"She was the Wicked Witch of the East," the old woman replied. "And I am the Witch of the North. I came here as fast as I could when I heard that she was dead."

"We do not have witches in Kansas," Dorothy said.

"The Land of Oz has four witches," the woman said. "Two of them, who live in the North and the South, are good. The other two, who live here in the East and in the West, are bad. I am not as powerful as the Wicked Witch of the East or I would have freed the Munchkins myself."

"The Land of Oz?" Dorothy asked in surprise. "Is that where I am?"

"Yes," the old woman said. "It is ruled by a great wizard named Oz. He is more powerful than the rest of us."

"Where is he?" Dorothy asked.

"He lives in the City of Emeralds," the old woman said. Suddenly, she began to laugh. "Look, the witch has melted away!" she cried. "Only her shoes are left. They are yours now. They have a magic charm, but I cannot remember what it is."

Dorothy picked up the silver shoes and put them on the table.

"I want to go back to my aunt and uncle now," she said. "Can you help me to find the way home?"

The Munchkins shook their heads.

"There is a terrible desert to the east," one said.

"There is a terrible desert to the south where the Quadlings live," said another.

"And a terrible desert to the west," said a third. "There the Wicked Witch of the West rules the yellow people called the Winkies. They are her slaves."

"The North is my home," the old woman said, "and it too is surrounded by desert. I'm afraid you will have to stay in the Land of Oz."

Dorothy began to cry. The good witch took off her cap and balanced the point on the end of her nose. "One, two, three!" she said.

The cap changed to a piece of slate. On it was written: *LET DOROTHY GO TO THE CITY OF EMERALDS*

"Is your name Dorothy, dear?" the old woman asked.

"Yes," Dorothy said. "Where is the city?"

"It is in the center of the Land of Oz," she replied.

"Is the Great Wizard a good man?" Dorothy asked.

"I have never seen him," the old woman explained, "but he is a good wizard. It is a long journey to reach him, and it will be dangerous."

"Please come with me," Dorothy begged.

The old woman shook her head. "I cannot," she said. She kissed Dorothy's forehead. "But nobody will harm a person who has been kissed by the Witch of the North. Now, look for a road made with yellow bricks. And when you get to the City of Emeralds, tell the wizard Oz what has happened. Goodbye, my dear."

The Good Witch of the North whirled around three times and vanished.

"Come on, Toto," Dorothy said. "We must get ready for our journey."

They ate and drank. Dorothy filled a basket with bread from the cupboard. She put on her blue and white checked dress and a sunhat, took off her old shoes, and put on the silver shoes. She locked the door of the house and put the key in her pocket.

Then Dorothy and Toto set off bravely to find the yellow brick road—the one that would take them all the way to the Wonderful Wizard of Oz.

CHAPTER TWO

The Yellow Brick Road

It was easy to find the right road—it was the only one paved with yellow bricks. How pretty the countryside was! The sun shone as Dorothy and Toto walked along, and the birds sang.

The Munchkins lived in round houses with domed roofs. They had heard that Dorothy had killed the Wicked Witch of the East, and they came out to see her as she walked past. That evening, as it grew dark, a Munchkin named Boq invited Dorothy to eat and spend the night with his family.

"You must be a great witch," he said. "You wear silver shoes, you have killed the witch—and you have white in your dress, which only good witches wear. And it is kind of you to wear blue too, because blue is the Munchkins' favorite color."

I am only an ordinary girl blown here by a tornado, Dorothy thought, *but they think I am a witch!*

The next morning, she got ready to set off with Toto again.

"How far is it to the City of Emeralds?" she asked Boq.

"I do not know," he replied. "I have never been there. But I know that it is a long way and that you must pass through many dangerous places to get there."

I cannot turn back now, Dorothy thought, *I need Oz's help to get to Kansas.*

She said goodbye to the Munchkins and set off once more down the yellow brick road. After walking a few miles, she decided to rest in a cornfield. Dorothy sat gazing at a scarecrow stuffed with straw and wearing blue Munchkin clothes. Suddenly, one of its eyes winked at her. Then it said, "Hello! How are you?"

"Did you speak?" Dorothy asked.

"Yes," the scarecrow replied. "How are you?"

"Very well, thank you," Dorothy said. "And how are you?"

"I'm not feeling well," the scarecrow replied, "perched up on this pole all day and all night."

"Can't you get down?" Dorothy asked.

"Not unless you take this pole away," he replied.

Dorothy reached up and lifted the scarecrow to the ground. He bowed and walked around her. "Who are you?" he asked.

"My name is Dorothy," she replied, "and I come from Kansas. I am going to ask the Wizard of Oz to help me go home."

"Who is Oz?" the Scarecrow asked. "You see, my head is stuffed with straw and I have no brains, none at all. Do you think the Wizard of Oz could give me some?"

"I don't know," Dorothy said, "but you are welcome to come with me."

They set off along the yellow brick road. As they walked, Dorothy told the Scarecrow all about the gray prairies of Kansas.

"I cannot understand why you want to leave this beautiful country to go back to such a dreary place," he said.

"That is because you have no brains," Dorothy teased him. "There is no place like home."

The road became rough and full of holes. Toto jumped over them, Dorothy walked around them—but the Scarecrow fell into them.

There were fewer houses, and the countryside was bleak and lonely, for there were no crops in the fields. It began to grow dark. At last they found a deserted cottage where they spent the night.

The next morning, as they set out on the road again, they heard a terrible groan. Dorothy crept forward, afraid. "I can see the sun shining on something bright in the trees!" she whispered.

She stopped suddenly and gasped in surprise. A man made of tin was standing by a tree with an axe in his hand. Toto barked and snapped at the man's legs, but the man did not move.

"Did you groan?" Dorothy asked politely.

"Yes," the Tin Man replied. "I have been standing here groaning for more than a year, and nobody has come to help me."

"How can *I* help you?" Dorothy asked.

The Tin Man told Dorothy to go to his little cottage and bring back his oil can. As soon as Dorothy had oiled his joints, he put down his axe and moved freely again.

"Thank you," he said. "You have saved my life. I left my oil can behind and was caught in a storm, which rusted me. But why are you here?"

When Dorothy told him her story, the Tin Man said, "I once had a heart, but now I have none. Do you think Oz could give me one?"

"I don't know," Dorothy said, "but you are welcome to come with us."

And soon Dorothy, Toto, the Scarecrow and the Tin Man were walking along the yellow brick road—and ready for any danger that might come their way.

CHAPTER THREE

A Cowardly Lion

"Why don't you have a heart?" the Scarecrow asked as they walked along.

"I became a woodman like my father," the Tin Man explained, "and I planned to marry a Munchkin girl who lived with an old woman nearby. This old woman did not want to lose the girl, so she asked the Wicked Witch of the East to stop the marriage."

"How did she do that?" Dorothy asked.

"She put a spell on my axe," he replied. "One day, when I was chopping wood, the axe fell and chopped off my leg. So the tinsmith made me a tin leg. The axe cut off my other leg, my arms, and my head. It split my body in two. The tinsmith replaced each part, and I thought I had beaten the witch. But I had no heart and I could no longer love my Munchkin girl."

"I should prefer to have brains," the Scarecrow said, "for a fool would not know what to do with a heart."

"Brains do not make a person happy," the Tin Man said, "and happiness is the best thing in the world."

Which of them is right? Dorothy asked herself. *I wish I could get back to Kansas to ask Aunt Em.*

Now Dorothy and her friends were walking through thick, dark woods. Sometimes they heard a deep growl, and Toto kept close to Dorothy's side. He did not even bark.

The Good Witch's kiss will keep me from harm, Dorothy thought, *and nothing can hurt the Tin Man and the Scarecrow. But I am afraid for Toto.*

From behind the trees came a terrible roar. Suddenly, an enormous lion leapt out in front of them. He pushed the

Scarecrow off the road and clawed at the Tin Man, knocking him over. Little Toto ran barking toward the lion. Dorothy, afraid that the lion would hurt Toto, slapped the lion hard on his nose.

"You should be ashamed of yourself!" she cried. "Attacking a man made of straw, a man made of tin, and this little animal. You're a coward!"

"I know," the lion said sadly. "What is that little animal?"

"He's my dog," Dorothy said. "Why are you such a coward when you're so big?"

"I think I was born that way," the lion replied. "All the other animals expect me to be brave because I am the King of the Beasts. I have learned to roar loudly, and that frightens everybody. But my heart beats fast whenever there is any danger."

"At least you have a heart," the Tin Man said. "I'm going to ask the Wizard of Oz to give me one."

"I'm going to ask him to give me brains," the Scarecrow said.

"I'm going to ask him how I can get home," Dorothy said.

"Do you think he could give me courage?" the Lion asked. "As long as I know that I'm a coward, I shall be unhappy."

"I do not know," Dorothy replied, "but you are welcome to come with us. You will help to scare away the other wild animals."

And once more, the little band of friends set off down the yellow brick road.

They slept under the trees that night and ate nuts and bread. When they had been walking less than an hour the next morning, they came to a big ditch that crossed the road. It was wide and deep with steep sides.

"What can we do?" Dorothy cried.

"We must stay here," the Scarecrow replied.

To their surprise, the Lion looked at the ditch and said, "I think I could jump over it. I could carry you all on my back. Who wants to be first?"

"Me!" the Scarecrow said. "A fall can't hurt *me*."

Soon they were all safely on the other side of the ditch, where they found themselves in a very dark and gloomy part of the forest.

"This is where the Kalidahs live," the Lion whispered. "They are great beasts with bodies like bears and heads like tigers. Their claws are so long and sharp that they could tear me in two. I'm afraid of them."

As the Lion spoke, they came to another ditch across the road. It was so wide that even the Lion could not jump it.

"There is a big tree over there," the Scarecrow said. "The Tin Man could cut it down to make a bridge for us."

"That's a good idea," the Lion said. "You must have *some* brains in your head."

The Tin Man set to work. When he had finished chopping, the Lion pushed the great trunk across the ditch. As they began to cross, the Kalidahs started running toward them. The Lion, who was last in the line, gave a roar so terrible that the beasts stopped.

But only for a moment! Then they began to move forward again.

"They will tear us to pieces now!" the Lion said to Dorothy. "Stand behind me. I shall fight back as long as I am alive."

CHAPTER FOUR

Deadly Poppies

"Quickly!" the Scarecrow called to the Tin Man. "Chop away the log at this end!"

The Tin Man raised his axe at once. Just as the Kalidahs had almost reached them, the tree trunk fell onto the rocks below, taking the two terrible beasts with it.

"My heart is beating fast," the Lion said.

"I wish I had a heart," the Tin Man replied.

They walked as quickly as they could through the rest of the forest until they came to a river. On the other side of the river, they could see the yellow brick road running through beautiful countryside full of flowers and fruit trees.

"The Tin Man must build us a raft," the Scarecrow said.

As the Tin Man used his axe, the others picked and ate the delicious fruit. It takes a long time to build a raft, and they had to sleep under the trees when darkness fell.

The next morning, the travelers were full of hope. The sun was shining, they had eaten well—and the raft was finished. Dorothy sat in the middle of the raft, holding Toto. The Scarecrow and the Tin Man stood together on one side with the heavy Lion on the other. Then they pushed the raft away from the bank with long poles.

But in the middle of the river, their poles could not reach the bottom of the water, and the strong current began to carry them away. The Scarecrow pushed so hard that his pole stuck in some mud and he was left clinging to it.

Once I was stuck on a pole in a cornfield, he thought, *but it is worse to be stuck on a pole in a river.*

The Tin Man began to cry—until he remembered that he might make himself rusty.

"I think I can swim to the bank on the other side," the Lion said. "I can pull the raft after me if you hold the tip of my tail."

He sprang into the water. It was hard work, but slowly the Lion pulled them toward the bank.

"How can we save the Scarecrow?" Dorothy asked.

The Lion and the Tin Man shook their heads. They were still sitting on the bank thinking when a stork flew past.

"Where are you going?" the stork asked them.

"To the Emerald City," Dorothy replied. "But we are wondering how to save our friend over there."

The stork looked. "I could bring him back myself if he wasn't so big and heavy," she said.

"He isn't!" Dorothy said. "He's very light because he's made of straw."

The stork flew over the river and picked up the Scarecrow in her great claws and carried him back to the bank.

They started along the yellow brick road again, listening to the birds singing, looking at the beautiful flowers. A clump of scarlet poppies caught Dorothy's eye, and she leaned over to breathe in their perfume. Soon they found themselves in a great field of poppies. Their scent was so strong that Dorothy's eyes began to close.

"If we leave her here, she will die," the Lion said. "The smell of these poppies is killing us all. Look! Toto is asleep now and my eyes are . . . clo . . . s . . .ing."

"Run, Lion!" the Scarecrow shouted. "The poppies cannot harm me or the Tin Man because we are made of straw and tin. We will carry Dorothy from this field, but you're too heavy to be carried."

The Lion ran as fast as he could. The others carried Dorothy and Toto from the field, following the bend of the river. At the edge of the field, they came across the Lion, fast asleep.

"We must leave him here," the Tin Man said sadly.

"I'm sorry," the Scarecrow said. "He was a good friend."

CHAPTER FIVE

The Emerald City

As the Scarecrow and the Tin Man waited for Dorothy to wake up, they heard a loud growl. A strange beast was rushing across the grass toward them.

It was a great yellow wildcat.

Its mouth was wide open, showing two rows of ugly teeth, and its eyes glowed like balls of fire. It was chasing a tiny gray field mouse. The Tin Man raised his axe and cut off the wildcat's head as it ran by.

"Thank you for saving my life!" the mouse squeaked.

"I help all those who need a friend, even if it is only a little mouse," the Tin Man replied.

"Only a *mouse*!" the animal cried. "I am a *queen*—the Queen of all Field Mice."

Several mice came running after their queen. "This funny tin man has saved my life," she said, "and from now on, we must obey his every wish."

Toto woke up and jumped at the mice, barking, but the Tin Man caught him in his arms.

"Can we do anything to help?" one of the mice asked.

"Oh, yes, you can save our friend, the Lion, who is asleep in the poppy field," the Tin Man replied.

"Send for all your mice, and tell each mouse to bring a piece of string," the Scarecrow said.

When Dorothy opened her eyes, she saw thousands of mice scampering toward the Lion. That is how they saved the King of the Beasts, by dragging him from the field of poppies. The Lion woke up and laughed to think that such tiny creatures had saved him.

Before they left, the Queen of the Mice handed Dorothy a small silver whistle. "If ever you need us again, call us. We shall come to help you. Goodbye!"

The friends set off again. The yellow brick road was smooth now. The fences and the houses were painted green, and the people wore green clothes and pointed hats.

"We must be close to the Emerald City," Dorothy said.

When they came to a farmhouse, Dorothy asked if they could spend the night there.

"What about the lion?" the farmer asked.

"He's tame—and he's a coward," Dorothy said.

They all went inside. The farmer's family was surprised to see such a strange group.

"We are going to see the Great Oz," Dorothy explained.

"Are you sure that Oz will see you?" the farmer asked.

Dorothy was surprised to learn that nobody in the Emerald City had ever seen the Wonderful Wizard of Oz.

"He never goes out," the farmer explained. "Nobody has ever seen him, not even his servants. He can take on any shape he wishes: a bird, a cat, an elephant. Nobody knows who the real Oz is."

"Oh dear," Dorothy said. "We must try to see him; otherwise we shall have made our long journey for nothing."

"Why do you want to see him?" the farmer asked.

"I want a heart," the Tin Man said.

"I want some brains," the Scarecrow said.

"I want some courage," the Lion said.

"And I want to go home," Dorothy finished.

"Well, Oz can do anything," the farmer said. "But the most difficult thing is to get in to see him first."

The next morning, as soon as the sun rose, they thanked the farmer and walked toward the green glow in the sky.

"That must be the Emerald City," Dorothy said.

By the afternoon, they had come to the great green wall around the city. In front of them, right at the end of the yellow brick road, was a big gate, studded with glittering emeralds. Dorothy pushed the bell, and the gate swung open. They walked into an arched room where the walls glistened with emeralds.

A man stood before them, dressed in green from head to toe. Even his skin was greenish. Next to him was a large green box.

"Why have you come to the Emerald City?" he asked.

"We came here to see the Great Oz," Dorothy replied.

The man was so surprised that he sat down.

"I am the Guardian of the Gate," he said, "and it has been many years since anybody asked to see Oz." He shook his head. "He is powerful and terrible." The Guardian looked straight at them. "If you have come here for no good reason, he will be angry . . . and he will destroy all of you with the blink of an eye."

CHAPTER SIX

Meeting Oz

"We have come here for a good reason," the Scarecrow said. "We have been told that Oz is a good wizard."

"Yes, he is," the Guardian of the Gate said, "and he rules the Emerald City wisely. But nobody has ever dared to ask to see him. Ah, well . . . since you have asked to see the Great Oz, I must take you to his palace. First, put on these spectacles. The brightness of the Emerald City will blind you."

He opened the big box and gave them each a pair of spectacles, which he locked around their heads with a key. Then he put on his own spectacles and led them into the streets of the Emerald City. The green marble houses dazzled them, and all the people were dressed in green.

They came to a big building in the middle of the city.

"This is the palace of the Wizard of Oz," the Guardian said. He turned to the green-bearded soldier guarding the door. "These strangers are asking to see Oz."

The soldier took a message to the Throne Room—to Oz himself. At last, he came back.

"Have you seen Oz?" Dorothy asked.

"Oh, no," the soldier replied, "but I spoke to him. He wanted to send you away until I told him that you had a mark on your forehead and you were wearing silver shoes. He will see you in the morning."

He blew a green whistle and a young girl came in. She showed them to pretty rooms with fountains in the center and shelves with green books. In the wardrobe was a green dress that fit Dorothy perfectly.

Dorothy was the first to visit the Wonderful Wizard of Oz.

When a bell rang, she entered the Throne Room.

It was a beautiful room. Emeralds glittered everywhere, lit by a great light as bright as the sun. In the middle of the room stood a throne. On it was an enormous head.

There were no arms. No legs. No body. No hair.

It had only eyes, a nose, and an enormous mouth.

As Dorothy gazed at it, afraid, the mouth opened. "I am Oz, the Great and Terrible," it said. "Who are you and why have you come here?"

"I am Dorothy, the Small and the Meek," she replied. "I have come for your help."

"Where did you get those silver shoes?" Oz asked.

"I got them from the Wicked Witch of the East," Dorothy explained. "My house killed her when it fell on her."

"Where did you get that mark on your forehead?"

"That is where the Good Witch of the North kissed me when she sent me to find you," Dorothy replied. "Please help me to go home to Kansas."

Oz stared hard at Dorothy. "In my country, you have to pay for what you get," he said. "If I use my magic powers to help you, you must help me in return."

"What must I do?" Dorothy asked.

"I want you to kill the Wicked Witch of the West," he replied. "She is the only wicked witch left in the Land of Oz. She has made the yellow Winkies her slaves."

Dorothy began to cry. "I have never killed anyone," she said. "And if you are a great wizard and cannot kill her, how would *I* do it?"

"I do not know," the Head replied. "But go and do what I ask and do not ask to see me again until you have done it."

Dorothy left the Throne Room and told her friends what Oz had said. Then she went to her room and cried herself to sleep.

When the Scarecrow went to see Oz, he found a beautiful lady sitting on the throne. The Tin Man found a roaring beast and the Lion found a ball of fire. Each shape gave the same command: Kill the Wicked Witch of the West!

"What shall we do?" Dorothy asked her friends sadly. "I do not want to kill anybody."

"We *have* to do it!" her friends replied. "We must go to the Land of the Winkies and kill her."

The Tin Man sharpened his axe for the journey and oiled his joints. The Scarecrow stuffed himself with fresh straw. The green girl filled Dorothy's basket with good things to eat. The green-bearded soldier led them to the gates of the Emerald City. The Guardian of the Gate unlocked their spectacles and opened the door for them.

"Which road leads to the Wicked Witch of the West?" Dorothy asked him.

"There is no road," he replied. "Nobody ever wants to go that way."

CHAPTER SEVEN

The Wicked Witch of the West

"But how will we find the wicked witch?" Dorothy asked.

"*She* will find *you* as soon as you enter the country of the Winkies," the Guardian explained. "She will make you her slaves, like them."

"No, she won't," the Scarecrow replied. "We are going to kill her."

"Be careful!" the man replied. "She is wicked and fierce. She will never allow you to kill her. Now keep to the west, where the sun sets."

They turned toward the west, walking across fields full of daisies and buttercups. To her surprise, Dorothy saw that her dress was now white—and so was Toto's ribbon. The ground became hilly. There were no crops and no farmhouses. It was hot too, for there were no trees to give them shade.

The Wicked Witch of the West had only one eye, but it was as powerful as a telescope. It could see everywhere and everything. As the Witch sat at the door of her castle, she saw Dorothy and Toto and the Lion lying asleep on the ground while the others kept watch. She blew her silver whistle angrily, and a pack of wolves came running up to her.

"Run and tear them to pieces," she commanded. "They are no use to me. One is a girl, another a lion—and the others are made of straw and of tin."

When the Scarecrow and the Tin Man saw the wolves coming, the Tin Man seized his axe.

"Get behind me!" he said to the Scarecrow. "This is *my* fight."

He killed them all—forty wolves—and the friends set off on their journey again.

This made the Wicked Witch of the West even angrier. She blew her silver whistle twice, and a flock of wild crows came toward her.

"Fly and peck them to pieces," she commanded.

When he saw the crows flying toward them, the Scarecrow said, "Lie down beside me. This is *my* fight."

He killed them all—forty of them—and the friends set off on their journey again.

The Wicked Witch of the West blew her silver whistle three times and a swarm of black bees flew toward her.

"Fly to them and sting them to death!" she commanded.

When the Scarecrow saw the bees flying toward them, he said to the Tin Man, "Take out my straw and spread it over everybody."

The bees flew at the Tin Man, but they didn't see the others, who were covered with straw. When the bees hit the hard tin, their stingers broke off, killing them. As soon as the others had stuffed the straw back into the Scarecrow, they all started on their journey again.

The Wicked Witch of the West was so angry that she stomped her feet and called twelve Winkie slaves to her. She gave them each a spear.

"Go and kill those strangers," she commanded.

But the Winkies were not brave. They crept closer and closer to Dorothy until the Lion roared. Then they ran back to the castle, where the Witch beat them with a strap.

"I shall have to use my Golden Cap now," she said to herself.

This Golden Cap had magic powers. Anyone who owned it could call up the Winged Monkeys for help—but only three times.

I have already called them twice before, the Witch thought. *This is my last chance, but I have no choice. Everything else has failed.*

The Wicked Witch took the Golden Cap from her cupboard and placed it on her head. Then she stood on her left foot and said: "*Ep-pe, pe-pe, kak-ke!*"

Then she stood on her right foot and said: "*Hil-lo, hol-lo, hel-lo!*"

Then while standing on both feet, she cried: "*Ziz-zy, zuz-zy, zik!*"

Now the charm began to work. The sky darkened, and a low rumbling filled the air. There was a rush of wings and a chattering and laughing. When the sun came out again, it lit up a crowd of monkeys with huge wings on their shoulders surrounding the Wicked Witch.

"Why have you called us?" their leader asked.

"There are strangers in my land," she told him. "Go and destroy them all except the lion. I have decided to put him to work in the fields like a horse."

"Your command shall be obeyed," he said.

And the monkey flew away with the others to Dorothy and her friends. Some of the monkeys seized the Tin Man and dropped him onto some rocks far away. Some monkeys caught hold of the Scarecrow and pulled out all his straw. Some tied ropes around the Lion and took him back to the Witch's castle.

But they did not harm Dorothy at all.

The leader of the Winged Monkeys flew up to her, stretching out his long hairy arms to take her. Then he saw the mark of the Good Witch of the North on her forehead.

"This girl is protected by the Power of Good," he shouted to the others, "and that is stronger than the Power of Evil. We will take her to the castle."

The Wicked Witch of the West knew that she could not harm Dorothy, so she put her to work in the kitchen. She looked at the mark on Dorothy's forehead, looked down at her silver shoes, and trembled with fear.

She does not understand how powerful her shoes are, the Witch thought. *I must get them for myself.*

But Dorothy never took off her shoes, except at night and when she took her bath. The Witch was terrified of the dark—and even more terrified of water.

So the Witch tricked Dorothy. She made Dorothy fall onto the kitchen floor and snatched up one of the shoes when it fell off. Now she had half the power.

"Give me back my shoe!" Dorothy shouted.

"I will not!" the Witch said.

Dorothy was so angry that she picked up a bucket of water and threw it over the Wicked Witch. To her horror and surprise, the Witch began to shrink. Then she melted into a brown, sticky mess with a silver shoe in the middle.

"The Wicked Witch of the West is dead!" Dorothy shouted to the Lion and to the Winkie slaves. "You are all free!"

Only one thought spoiled her happiness that day. What had happened to the Scarecrow and the Tin Man?

CHAPTER EIGHT

An Ordinary Man

Dorothy and the Lion asked some of the Winkies to help them rescue their friends. They traveled for almost two days until they came to the rocky plain where the Tin Man lay. He was battered and bent, and his axe was rusty. The Winkies carried him gently back to the castle.

"Are any of your people tinsmiths?" Dorothy asked.

They nodded and brought tools to mend him. For three days, they hammered and bent and pounded. They fitted a new golden handle to his axe, and its polished blade shone like silver. At last, the Tin Man was as good as new. He walked to Dorothy's room and thanked her.

"If only we had the Scarecrow with us again," he wept.

Dorothy wept, too. "We must try to find him," she said.

She called the Winkies to help her. They walked for almost two days until they came to a tall tree. Up in its branches they saw the Scarecrow's clothes. The Tin Man chopped down the tree, and they carried the clothes back to the castle. They stuffed them with clean straw. At last, the Scarecrow was as good as new.

"We have killed the Wicked Witch of the West, just as the Wizard of Oz asked us," Dorothy said. "Now it is time to go back to the Emerald City and make him keep *his* promise."

"I shall get my heart," the Tin Man said.

"I shall get my brains," the Scarecrow said.

"I shall get my courage," the Lion said.

"And I shall go back home," Dorothy said.

They set off the next day. Dorothy filled her basket with food from the witch's cupboard for the journey. There she found the Golden Cap, and she decided to wear it instead of her old sunbonnet.

Day after day they walked through yellow daisies and buttercups—and still they did not see the poppy fields ahead.

We are lost! Dorothy thought.

Then she remembered the silver whistle the Queen of the Mice had given her. She blew hard. In a few minutes, the mice came pattering toward them.

"Can you show us the way back to Oz?" Dorothy asked.

The Queen looked at the Golden Cap on Dorothy's head. "Why don't you call the Winged Monkeys?" she asked. "They will fly you to the Land of Oz in less than an hour. You only have to repeat the words written inside it."

"I didn't know," Dorothy said in surprise.

She repeated the charm, and the Winged Monkeys appeared. In less than an hour, they were flying above the shining walls of the Emerald City. The monkeys put them down outside the gates, bowed, and flew off again. The Guardian of the Gate was surprised to see them, but he took the news of the Wicked Witch's death straight to the Wizard of Oz.

The wizard did not reply.

They waited for three days. At last the Scarecrow became impatient.

"Tell Oz," he said, "that if he does not keep his promise or let us see him, we shall call the Winged Monkeys."

The Wizard of Oz was so frightened by this message that he sent for them all the next day. But when they went into the Throne Room, there was nobody there.

A loud voice called from the dome: "I am Oz, the Great and the Terrible," it said. "Why have you come to see me?"

"We have come to claim our promise," Dorothy replied.

"Is the Wicked Witch of the West really dead?" the voice asked.

"Yes!" Dorothy said.

"Come back tomorrow!" the voice commanded them.

"No!" they all cried. "You must keep your promise *now*."

The Lion decided to frighten the Wizard with a loud roar. Toto jumped up and ran away, knocking over a wooden screen in the corner of the room. Behind it stood a little old man with a bald head and wrinkled face.

"Who are you?" the Tin Man cried.

"I am Oz, the Great and Terrible," the man replied in a trembling voice.

Dorothy and her friends looked at him in dismay.

"So you are not a great wizard?" Dorothy asked.

"No, I'm afraid not," he replied. "I'm just an ordinary man."

CHAPTER NINE

Oz Flies Away

The Wizard of Oz led them to a small room behind the Throne Room.

"You will be the only ones who will ever know what I really am," he said. "Look! You must know the truth."

In the corner of the room lay a great head with a painted face and the dress and mask of the lovely lady. The beast was just skins sewn together. As for the Ball of Fire—it was a ball of cotton, set on fire with oil.

"I used to be a ventriloquist," Oz said, "so I can throw my voice wherever I wish."

"You should be ashamed of yourself," the Scarecrow said. "What are you doing in the Land of Oz?"

"I used to work for a circus in Omaha," he replied. "I flew in a hot-air balloon at the entrance to attract people. One day, I didn't come down again. I drifted until I came to this beautiful country. The people thought I was a great wizard. They did anything I asked. So I told them to build this city and this palace. I made them put on green spectacles so everything looked green. But I am afraid of the witches here. They have great power—and I have none."

"So you asked me to kill one of them," Dorothy said. "You are a very wicked man."

"Oh, no, I'm a good man," he replied, "but a bad wizard."

"Can't you give me brains?" the Scarecrow asked.

"You only learn by doing," Oz replied. "You have to know how to use your brains—and you have already done that. But come back tomorrow and I shall give you some."

"Can you give me courage?" the Lion asked.

"You have plenty of courage," Oz replied. "Every living creature is afraid when it faces danger. Courage lies in facing danger when you are afraid—and you have already done that. But come back tomorrow, and I shall give you some courage."

"Can you give me a heart?" the Tin Man asked.

"A heart makes most people unhappy," Oz replied. "You are lucky not to have one. But come back tomorrow, and I shall give you one."

"Can you get me back home?" Dorothy asked.

"I shall need a few days to think about that," Oz said. "I shall do my best to help you all if you will keep my secret."

The next morning, Oz called in the Scarecrow. He took the straw from his head and filled it with corn bran—bran-new brains, he called it. And the Scarecrow felt wiser.

Oz called in the Tin Man. He cut a hole in his tin chest and placed a silk heart inside. And the Tin Man felt kinder.

Oz called in the Lion. He gave him a drink from a beautiful green bottle. And the Lion felt braver.

"I have given them all what they thought they needed," Oz said to himself. "But it will be a little harder to carry Dorothy back to Kansas. I'm not sure how I can do that."

For three days, Dorothy heard nothing from Oz. Her friends were happy now, but she was still sad. On the fourth day, Oz sent for her.

"I came to this country by balloon," he said, "and you came in a tornado. So you must leave by air. I cannot make a tornado, but I can make a balloon. We shall use hot air to float it." He looked at Dorothy. "I don't like being shut in my palace all day," he said. "Can I come back with you?"

Dorothy nodded. They started to make the balloon right

away from strips of green silk, which they tied to a big clothes basket.

News spread quickly inside the Emerald City, and everybody came to see the wonderful sight. The Tin Man lit a large fire, and the balloon swelled with hot air. Oz climbed into the basket.

"I am going to visit my brother wizard who lives in the clouds," he said to his people. "The Scarecrow will rule you while I'm away. Come on, Dorothy! Get in!"

But as Dorothy went to find Toto, the balloon began to tug at its ropes. Suddenly, it rose into the air without her.

"Come back!" she screamed. "I want to come with you!"

That was the last they saw of the Wonderful Wizard of Oz. Dorothy wept bitterly.

"How will I get home now?" she cried.

Chapter Ten

Home Again

The Scarecrow tried to persuade Dorothy to stay in the Land of Oz.

"No, I want to go home!" Dorothy cried.

"You could call the Winged Monkeys to take you," he replied.

But the Winged Monkeys could not help because they could not go beyond their own land.

"Let us ask the green-bearded soldier," the Scarecrow said.

"Glinda might be able to help you," the soldier said. "She is the Witch of the South. She rules over the Quadlings and she is the most powerful witch of all. The road to her castle is straight to the south."

"I think we should go there," the Scarecrow said.

"I will come with you," the Tin Man said.

"Me too," the Lion said. "I can protect you from the wild animals."

The sun shone brightly as the friends turned toward the Land of the South. Dorothy was full of hope again. Soon they came to a forest. As the Scarecrow was walking past a large tree, a branch picked him up and pushed him back. The same happened to the Lion. But the Tin Man chopped off the branch, and they all passed safely by.

At last they came to a high white wall that seemed to be made of china. The Tin Man made a ladder for them. They gasped in surprise as they reached the top. In front of them stretched countryside of smooth white china, like an enormous plate. There were houses and farms, people and animals—all made of china and all no higher than Dorothy's knee.

They jumped from the wall and walked carefully through the country of china people. Everybody ran out of their way, afraid that the strangers would knock them over and break them. After about an hour, they reached another wall at the other end of the country. It was not so high and they jumped over easily, although the Lion's tail smashed a china church.

They walked through rough countryside full of bogs and marshes and tall grass, until they came to another forest.

"This is a beautiful forest," the Lion said. "I would like to live here."

As they reached an opening in the forest, they met hundreds of animals: tigers, elephants, bears, wolves, and foxes. The others were afraid, but the Lion said that the animals were just having a meeting. As they came close, the biggest of the tigers came up to them.

"Welcome, King of the Beasts," he said to the Lion. "You have come in time to bring peace again to all the animals of the forest. A terrible enemy threatens us—a monster spider who eats everything in sight. I'm glad you are here."

"If I kill it, will I be your King?" the Lion asked.

"Yes," the tiger growled. "It's sleeping in that oak tree over there."

The Lion killed the creature as it slept. With one blow of his paw, he knocked its head off. Then he promised to return to the forest when Dorothy was safely on her way home.

When they left the forest, they came to a steep rocky hill. They started to climb it, but a harsh voice called out, "Go away! Nobody is allowed to climb *our* hill!"

A man stepped out from the rock—the strangest man they had ever seen. He had a big head held up by a wrinkled neck and no arms. As they continued climbing anyway, his neck stretched out and his head struck the Scarecrow and send him tumbling down the hill. Hundreds of other strange men stood up behind the rocks, laughing.

"Call the Winged Monkeys!" the Tin Man told Dorothy.

Dorothy used the Golden Cap for the last time. The Winged Monkeys carried them safely to the country of the Quadlings. It seemed a rich and happy place. Corn ripened in the fields. The houses and fences were painted red, and the people were all dressed in red.

As they came close to the Castle of Glinda, a young girl took Dorothy to a room, where she washed her hands and face and combed her hair. The Lion shook the dust from his mane, the Scarecrow patted himself into his best shape, and the Tin Man polished himself and oiled his joints.

The Witch of the South was sitting on a throne of rubies. She was beautiful and young and her hair was red. Dorothy told her the story: how the tornado had brought her to the Land of Oz, how she had met her friends, and what adventures they had had.

"But my greatest wish is to go back to Kansas," Dorothy said. "My Aunt Em will think that something terrible has happened to me."

The witch Glinda kissed her. "I can tell you how to reach home," she said, "if you will give me the Golden Cap."

"Yes," Dorothy said. "It is of no use to me now."

"What will you do?" Glinda asked the Scarecrow.

"I wish to return as ruler of the Emerald City," he said. "I like it and the people like me. But how shall I get past those strange men on the hill?"

"I shall ask the winged Monkeys to take you there," Glinda replied. She turned to the Tin Man. "What will become of you?"

"The Winkies were very kind to me," he replied. "If I could

get back to the Country of the West, I should like to rule them."

"I shall ask the Winged Monkeys to take you there," Glinda replied. She looked at the Lion. "What about you?"

"I shall go back to the forest and become King of the Beasts," he replied.

"Then my third wish of the Golden Cap shall be that," Glinda said. "The Winged Monkeys will take you there."

"How shall I get back to Kansas?" Dorothy asked.

"Your silver shoes will carry you over the desert," Glinda replied. "If you had known how powerful they were, you could have returned the very first day."

"But I would still be in a cornfield without my brains!" the Scarecrow said.

"I would have rusted in a forest and never had my heart!" the Tin Man cried.

"I would have lived a coward forever," the Lion said.

Dorothy was glad to see her friends so happy, but all she wanted was to go home. She kissed her friends, said goodbye to the witch Glinda, and picked up Toto. Then she tapped the heels of her shoes together three times, as Glinda told her, and shouted: "Take me home to Aunt Em!"

The silver shoes took three steps. Suddenly Dorothy was swirling through the air. Then she found herself rolling over and over in the grass, barefoot because the wind had blown off the silver shoes. When she stopped rolling, she was next to the new farmhouse Uncle Henry had built after the tornado. Aunt Em was running toward her, shouting, "Where in the world have you come from, dear child?"

"From the Land of Oz," Dorothy replied. "Oh, Aunt Em, I'm *so* glad to be home again."